Cities through Time

Daily Life in Ancient and Modern

MOSCOW

by Patricia Toht

illustrations by Bob Moulder

RP

Runestone Press/Minneapolis
An imprint of Lerner Publishing Group

The *Cities through Time* series is produced by Runestone Press, an imprint of Lerner Publishing Group, in cooperation with Greenleaf Publishing, Inc., Geneva, Illinois.

Cover design by Michael Tacheny
Text design by Jean DeVaty and Melanie Lawson

Runestone Press
An imprint of Lerner Publishing Group
241 First Avenue North
Minneapolis, MN 55401 U.S.A.

Website address: www.lernerbooks.com

Library of Congress Cataloging-in-Publication Data

Toht, Patricia, 1960–
      Daily life in ancient and modern Moscow / by Patricia Toht ;
   illustrations by Bob Moulder.
         p.   cm. — (Cities through time)
      Includes index.
      Summary: A historical exploration of events and daily life in Moscow in both ancient and modern times.
      ISBN 0-8225-3220-4 (lib. bdg. : alk. paper)
      1. Moscow (Russia)—Social life and customs—Juvenile literature.
   2. Moscow (Russia)—History—Juvenile literature. [1. Moscow (Russia).]
   I. Moulder, Bob, ill. II. Title. III. Series.
   DK600.T64   2001
   957'.31—dc21   00-020347

Manufactured in the United States of America
1 2 3 4 5 6 – JR – 06 05 04 03 02 01

Contents

Introduction

Moscow is the capital of Russia, the largest country in the world. One of the world's largest cities, Moscow is home to nine million people. The modern-day city spreads over 339 square miles. But Moscow was once a small village on the banks of the Moskva (Moscow) River. At the heart of Moscow, visitors find the Kremlin. In modern times, the Kremlin is the seat of Russia's government.

Many years ago, the Kremlin was a fortress that safeguarded the people of Moscow. Its impressive red brick walls and nineteen elegant towers surround cathedrals, palaces, and bell towers. Colorful Saint Basil's Cathedral stands just outside the Kremlin walls. Over the centuries, as the city grew in size, some Muscovites (people of Moscow) came to live far from the secure walls of the Kremlin. To stay safe, they built walls even farther from the Kremlin.

The area occupied by the Kremlin is only a small part of modern Moscow, which expanded in rings. The old defensive walls have been replaced with roads and railroad tracks. And Moscow continues to grow. Yet the roads of the city all lead back to the Kremlin, the very site where the great city of Moscow had its beginnings.

RUSSIA

Moscow

Moscow River

NORTH ATLANTIC OCEAN

RUSSIA

N

— Current border

(Above, right) Gilded domes stand in sharp contrast to the hastily built apartment buildings and industrial smokestacks of Moscow.

Built for Czar Ivan the Terrible, colorful Saint Basil's Cathedral *(left)* symbolizes Moscow to the world.

No one knows what name the early people of Moscow gave to their settlement.

Timber was traded and used to build boats.

Settlers hunted wild game for food and traded the valuable pelts and meat.

6

Village on a Hill

Artifacts from the first settlements in the forests around Moscow date to 3000 B.C. By 1000 B.C., Finnish people lived in wooden huts in the forests. Around A.D. 500, the eastern Slavs migrated northward from the fertile grasslands known as the steppes. The Slavs lived in clans—groups of family members headed by an elder—and peacefully built clusters of wooden houses among the Finns.

The settlers cleared some forest to make small fields. Cattle helped pull wooden plows through the sandy soil. Farmers planted grain and hay. But the harvests were usually small because the soil wasn't very fertile. People fished in the rivers and hunted and trapped wild game in the woods.

The settlers traded many of their goods with people in nearby cities. In warm months, some settlers hauled their trade goods in horse-drawn carts northeastward to Novgorod or southeastward to Kiev. Some traders visited Constantinople, the capital of the Byzantine Empire. Others loaded their goods onto flat-bottomed boats and poled down rivers to trade with merchants in Asian cities. In cold months, horses pulled wooden sledges, or sleighs, full of trade goods across the ice and snow. In the cities, the settlers traded their wood, turpentine, wax, tar, meat, and honey for grain, cloth, metal, wine, and perfume.

These early people of Moscow worshiped nature gods. They believed that trees, plants, rocks, streams, and animals contained spirits. They performed sacrifices to obtain blessings. A medicine man, or shaman, practiced religious and healing rituals.

Unifying the Slavs

When clans of eastern Slavs settled in Moscow, other Slavic clans made new homes across a region stretching from Novgorod to Kiev. But fighting frequently broke out among the clans as each tried to seize neighboring land. The people of Novgorod sought a solution to the fighting. They traded with the Varangians, warrior-traders from Scandinavia. In A.D. 862, they invited the Varangian chieftain Rurik to rule over them and to bring order to the Slavs. Rurik's successor, Oleg, expanded his rule southward to Kiev in A.D. 879. He united the land between the two cities into a new kingdom called Kievan Rus. Its inhabitants became Russians. Kievan Rus extended from Novgorod to Kiev and included Moscow. The Grand Prince of All Rus ruled his subjects from Kiev. He divided Kievan Rus into small territories, each ruled by a prince who reported to the Grand Prince.

With the land of Kievan Rus united under one ruler, Oleg's successor, Vladimir, tried to unite the Russians under one religion. He focused on the Christian faith, which was then divided between the Roman Catholic Church of Rome and the Eastern Orthodox Church of Constantinople. Vladimir chose to follow the Eastern Orthodox faith. In A.D. 988, he ordered all his subjects to be baptized according to the Orthodox Church's rituals, and the Eastern Orthodox faith became the official religion of Russia. The head of the Russian Orthodox Church, called the metropolitan, resided in Kiev.

The Eastern Orthodox religion was gradually accepted by the Russians. To help spread the new religion, the Orthodox clergy spoke in Church Slavonic, a language that was based upon the related languages of the Slavs. Religious literature was translated into Cyrillic, a new alphabet for writing Slavic languages. But despite these efforts, the secret worship of traditional gods continued for centuries.

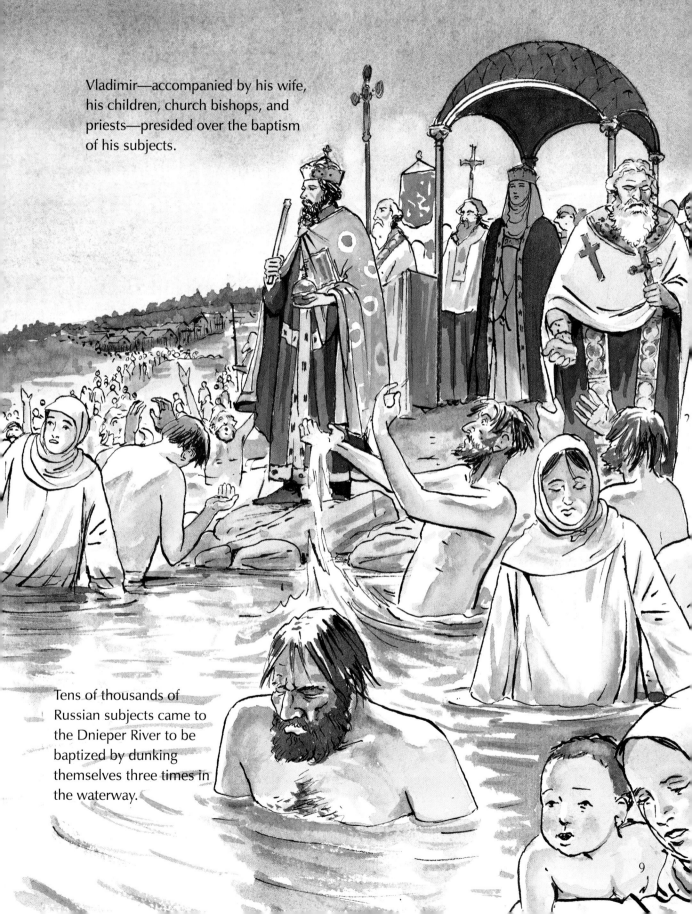

Vladimir—accompanied by his wife, his children, church bishops, and priests—presided over the baptism of his subjects.

Tens of thousands of Russian subjects came to the Dnieper River to be baptized by dunking themselves three times in the waterway.

The First Kremlin

According to legend, Kuchko, a fur trapper in the early 1100s, claimed land along the Moskva River. Kuchko's clan built a village of wooden huts on a hill near the spot where two streams, the Neglinnaya and the Yauza, emptied into the Moskva. Kuchkovo, as the village was called, became a trading post. And travelers journeying over land or down the Moskva River could rest in a villager's wooden home.

Prince Yuri Dolgoruky, the ruler of the territory around Kuchkovo, murdered Kuchko and confiscated the town and the surrounding lands. Prince Yuri then renamed the village Moscow, after the Moskva River.

Subjects of Prince Yuri help build a 4,000-foot-long fence around his settlement.

The first historical mention of Moscow appears in the *Ipatievskaya*, a twelfth-century document compiled by Orthodox monks, (members of the Orthodox Church who lived in a monastery). The document states that in the year 1147, Prince Yuri sent an invitation to another prince saying, "Come to me, brother, to Moscow."

By that time, Prince Yuri had added a warehouse, a church, and several other buildings to the hilltop settlement. In 1156 he built a 4,000-foot-long wooden stockade around the village. The growing village had become a fort, or *kreml* (kremlin). Huts surrounded the fort. Peasants and craftspeople hid within the Kremlin's walls in times of danger.

The hilltop location of Prince Yuri's fort, or kremlin, helped repel invaders.

The Mongol Yoke

The Mongols, a people of eastern central Asia, were among the most successful conquerors in history. Batu Khan (grandson of the Mongol conqueror Genghis Khan) led Mongol warriors in an invasion of Russia in the early 1200s. By 1237 the Mongol soldiers had reached Moscow and had burned the town. The invaders looted Moscow and moved on to conquer other Russian cities.

Known as the Golden Horde, the Mongol invaders controlled Moscow for more than two hundred years. Russians referred to this period of domination as the Mongol Yoke. The Mongols allowed local Russian princes to rule, but the princes remained under the control of the Mongol khan (leader).

The khans allowed the Russian people to keep their traditions. Moscow's citizens, for example, continued speaking their own

The Russians called the invading Mongol army the Golden Horde, after the large, gold-colored tent of the khan.

language and practicing their own customs and religion throughout the Mongol Yoke.

At the same time, however, the Mongols forced Russian men to serve in the Mongol army or as slaves. In this way, the Mongols made sure that Russian men could not take back their land through armed revolts. The Mongols also forced Russians to pay a tribute, or tax, that Russian tax collectors gathered each year. People usually gave up 10 percent of the money, food, fur, and other goods in their possession. The Mongols destroyed towns and killed people who refused to pay the tax.

The people of Moscow paid the tribute and did not cause trouble. For this reason, the city was allowed to grow in size and wealth. Over time, nearby villages along the Moskva River became part of the expanding city of Moscow.

The Mongols built roads and protected the trade routes leading into Moscow. The city became a thriving trade center, and the khan collected even more tribute from Moscow's citizens.

Mongol warriors rode short, sturdy ponies and used their archery skills to destroy Moscow's villages.

The fourteenth-century cleric Sergius
oversees the construction of a monk's cell
and of a church on the banks of the
Kantchoura River near Moscow (above).
A twelfth-century icon (facing page)
portrays Saint George.

Moscow, the Third Rome

In 1327 the head of the Russian Orthodox Church moved from Kiev to Moscow. Within the Kremlin, Russia's first stone church was constructed to mark the city's new status as a spiritual center. In 1453 Turkish invaders conquered the city of Constantinople and introduced the religion of Islam. As a result of this change, Constantinople was no longer the center of the Eastern Orthodox Church. Moscow claimed the title of the "Third Rome"—the new center of the Eastern Orthodox Church.

Moscow's church clergy divided into two groups. The white clergy were married parish priests. The higher-ranking black clergy were unmarried monks and bishops. Members of the white clergy usually wore black robes and small cylindrical hats. On special religious occasions, they wore robes of velvet or silk embroidered in gold or silver. The black clergy wore tall caps called miters, with veils that fell over their backs. They carried jeweled staffs to show their authority. All clergy wore beards.

The people of Moscow were summoned early to worship by the ringing of church bells. In church the men stood on the right, and the women stood on the left. Everyone held a candle for light.

The Russian Orthodox Church discouraged artists from making sculptures, which could be viewed as idols (false gods). Instead, artists made beautiful icons, or paintings of religious scenes and figures. Most Russians were illiterate (unable to read), so the icons helped them learn about the Bible. The Russian Orthodox Church relied on the icons, with their religious scenes and biblical figures, as a form of communication for the worshipers.

Icons were painted on wooden backgrounds. Artists hand-ground pigments, which they used to make colorful paints. They made white from lead, black from ash, and red from mercury. They used real gold to color halos and rich ornaments. Boiled linseed oil coated the icons, giving them a golden tone. The linseed oil also helped protect the paintings from being coated in black soot from the burning candles. Icons were not only for church use. People also kept icons in their homes, and warriors carried the sacred images into battle.

Rise of the Czars

The fourteenth and fifteenth centuries were a time of relative peace and prosperity in Moscow. But the land west of Moscow had been held in bondage by the Mongols, isolating the city from European culture. While nearby Europe experienced the Renaissance, a period of cultural and social transformation, Moscow remained unchanged under Mongol rule. But the power of the Golden Horde gradually weakened. In 1480 Russia's first national king, Ivan III, known as Ivan the Great, refused to pay Moscow's tribute to the Mongols. Moscow finally cast off Mongol control.

Under the leadership of Ivan the Great, Moscow grew to be Russia's capital and one of the largest cities in the world. The population increased to one hundred thousand people. From 1462 to 1505, Ivan took control of more land, eventually tripling the territory around Moscow, which came to be known as the Land of Muscovy.

Ivan expanded trade and welcomed foreign embassies (representatives of other countries) to Moscow. He sent a mission to Europe to hire architects, engineers, and craftspeople to help construct stone churches and the white stone walls and towers of the Kremlin. To support this transformation of Muscovy, Ivan taxed his citizens heavily.

Ivan the Great was the first Russian ruler to call himself czar, which comes from the Latin word *caesar*. He used this title to enhance his importance and to show his status as the one absolute ruler of Russia. He enforced his laws by severely punishing anyone who disobeyed his rules.

Ivan the Great introduced the *pomeste* system to gain the support of the upper class in Moscow. Under this system, individuals were assigned land in exchange for a pledge of military or administrative service to the czar. Such landowners were known as boyars. The peasants living on the land became tenant farmers or servants under the boyars.

The boyars of Moscow lived on estates in and around the city. Their multistoried wooden homes were heated by large porcelain stoves. Elegantly furnished rooms had fine wooden tables, chairs, and beds. Rich Oriental rugs often covered the floors. The boyars had servants who cooked their meals and cleaned their homes. The boyars also hired minstrels to provide music on stringed instruments for their entertainment.

Dressed to Kill

Moscow's landowning boyars dressed in long gowns drawn in at the waist by a belt. Over the gowns, the boyars wore dark capes of brocade or velvet trimmed in gold cord and fur. They sported fur-trimmed hats and soft high boots made of goatskin that was dyed yellow, red, or blue.

Refusing to yield to the Mongols' domination, Czar Ivan the Great (*above and inset*) dramatically tears up a letter from the Mongol ruler.

This twentieth-century painting shows the weary lives of Russia's peasants.

So Many Peasants

Most people living in and around Moscow during the rise of the czars were peasants who lived and worked on the boyars' estates. Some peasants farmed and tended animals. Others, called state peasants, lived on government- or church-owned land. During the winter, when farmwork let up, they made cloth, pottery, or furniture. Other peasants worked year-round as servants in the boyars' houses. Peasants had contracts with their landlords, who loaned the peasants money, grain, or tools in exchange for work. Peasants who paid off their contracts were free to leave, but few ever achieved this goal. State peasants paid lower taxes and had the freedom to buy land.

Peasants lived in *izbas*, one-room houses made of stacked logs with earthen floors and thatched roofs. The peasants stuffed moss into the cracks between the logs to keep in heat. Each izba had a small front yard with a high gate that might be decorated with wooden carvings.

The izbas were plainly furnished. On one wall was a clay stove for cooking and heating. A small hole in the roof vented the smoke. Peasants slept on planks by the stove during the long cold winters. Tables and benches were the only pieces of furniture. Shelves on the walls held kitchen utensils and a few possessions. Clothing hung on wall hooks.

In a corner of the izba, a table displayed the family's icons. Small oil lamps or candles burned continuously in front of the sacred iamges. Each time the peasants left and returned to the izba, they bowed before the icons, made the sign of the cross, and said a prayer to a saint.

The peasants' simple diet consisted of rye bread, buckwheat porridge, vegetables, and occasionally meat or fish. The vegetables came from their own small gardens, where peasants grew cucumbers, cabbages, carrots, turnips, and parsnips. Peasants usually began their day with a mug of milk or kvass, a drink made from fermented rye and fruit.

In the summertime, peasants dressed in clothing made of homespun linen. They didn't wear socks or stockings, but instead they wrapped their legs with strips of linen. Their shoes, called *lapti*, were woven from birch bark. In winter, peasants wore woolen clothes, sheepskin coats, fur caps with earflaps, and felt boots. The heavy clothes helped to keep them warm during bitter Moscow winters.

Pinewood was readily available in the forests of northern Russia. It was easily cut and shaped by artisans.

Building Boom

While Moscow grew in population, building boomed. The Muscovites built new homes and churches out of timber. Fire often broke out because candles and oil lamps were used for light. People couldn't carry enough water from wells or the river to fight the flames. To keep a fire from spreading to other buildings, the Muscovites tore down neighboring houses, which were rebuilt after the fire.

Ivan the Great encouraged stone architecture in the wooden city because stone structures could withstand fire. He also believed that the more permanent stone structures symbolized the wealth and power of Russia.

Ivan hired Italian architects to design the center of the Kremlin and oversaw the construction of a royal palace. Workers built the Kremlin's walls and towers and dug a moat (water channel). Foreign architects helped build or rebuild many of

Olearius, an ambassador to Moscow, described the foreign quarter as "a miniature segment of western Europe transplanted to the north-eastern outskirts of Moscow."

Moscow's cathedrals, which often had cupolas (rounded domes). Designers modified the shape to help shed snow in the winter. Skilled craftspeople built the domes out of pine, interlocking the pieces of wood without nails.

While the people of Moscow were happy to have foreigners work in the city, they were also fearful of them. Moscow had often been threatened with foreign invasion. The people grew suspicious of the growing population of foreigners whom Muscovites considered "unbelievers" and a danger to the Russian Orthodox Church. To calm local fears, the czars required all foreigners to live in a specific quarter of Moscow called the Nemetskaya Sloboda.

The French, Dutch, English, Italian, Scotch, and German residents of Nemetskaya Sloboda kept their native languages, customs, and styles of dress. Education was important to the foreigners, so many schools dotted the foreign quarter.

To Market

The busiest and most crowded section of Moscow was Red Square, a center of political and social life. In Red Square, czars delivered speeches, and church leaders blessed the people. Government criers announced new edicts (orders) and important news. Unemployed priests wandered the square offering their services to merchants and to boyars with private chapels. Scribes sold their works, jugglers and musicians entertained the crowds, and beggars asked for money. Red Square was also the site of public floggings (beatings) and even hangings of criminals.

A marketplace called the Kitay Gorod bordered Red Square. The rows of canopied stalls were grouped together according to the goods the merchants sold. People could buy silk and cloth, gold and silver, icons, saddles, shoes, clothing, furs, hats, pottery, and fruits and vegetables, each in its own area of the market. The people called one section of the Kitay Gorod the "lousy" market. There vendors sold old clothes, furniture, and junk. Barbers cut hair and trimmed men's beards.

Wednesdays and Fridays were the busiest days. From early morning on, the streets were filled with carts, produce wagons, and horses. Goods and coins quickly exchanged hands. Russian coins (kopeks and rubles) were very small, made of silver and gold, and round or oblong in shape. They slipped so easily through the fingers that many people resorted to carrying them in their mouths. At midday, vendors in the Kitay Gorod sold *pierogis* (small meat pies) to customers and merchants. After their meal, the shopkeepers napped in front of their booths. Selling started again in the afternoon. At dusk, shops were shuttered, booths taken down, and the gates to the Kitay Gorod closed for the night.

Wide muddy streets were
lined with logs to allow
shoppers and carts to pass.

Troubled Times

Ivan the Great called himself czar, but in 1547 his grandson Ivan IV was the first Russian ruler actually to be crowned czar. Ivan IV, also known as Ivan the Terrible, accomplished many things in the early years of his reign. He established a new legal code and made military improvements. He set up the first printing presses in Moscow and brought in foreign doctors, teachers, and artists to serve him.

Ivan IV established an important trade relationship with England. He enlarged his empire by expanding into Siberia, a vast expanse of land in northern Asia. He also ordered the building of a new church, Saint Basil's Cathedral, to commemorate his grandfather's defeat of the Mongols.

As Ivan the Terrible grew older, he turned against his advisers and the boyars of Moscow. He set up a black-hooded police force, the *oprichniki*, to carry out his wishes. Anyone suspected of plotting against him was executed in Red Square. He ordered thousands to be killed. He even murdered his own son in a fit of rage.

After the death of Ivan the Terrible in 1584, Moscow fell on hard times. This period came to be known as the Time of Troubles. Left without a ruler, various groups competed for the throne. Civil wars broke out in the countryside, and many boyars abandoned their land. Droughts and widespread crop failures led to years of famine (food shortages). An outbreak of plague killed many more people. In the early 1600s, more than one hundred thousand Muscovites died.

Seeing an opportunity in Moscow's weakness, Polish invaders threatened to take over the czar's throne. In 1612 the Russians united against the enemy and formed a national army, which defeated the Poles. A year later, a national assembly elected Mikhail Romanov, the grandnephew of Ivan IV, to assume the throne.

Mikhail Romanov and his successors brought peace to Moscow but didn't improve the lives of the peasants. Laws passed in 1649 made peasants into serfs who were no longer allowed to leave the boyars' estates. Because they owed their masters money, crops, and labor, poverty and starvation were common.

Famines in Moscow drove peasants to desperate measures. They used the thatch on their roofs to feed their starving livestock (right).

The Russian czar Ivan the Terrible *(right)* was responsible for many improvements to Moscow. But he also ordered the execution of thousands of his subjects.

Noblewomen used gold and silver thread to embroider designs of flowers and birds on their blouses, gowns, and velvet hats.

Punish your son in his youth, and he will give you a quiet old age....If you love your son, punish him frequently, that you may rejoice later.
　　　　—A rule from the Domostoi

Noblewomen

From the time of the Mongol Yoke through the late 1600s, wives of Moscow's boyars lived in a section of the house called the *terem*. This section was usually located on the upper floors or in the attic of the house.

In the terem, upper-class women sewed, sang, and painted. They did not dance or read books. Some homes had a private chapel, so that women would not have to go out in public to attend religious services. When the women did venture out from the terem, they wore long veils or hoods of white felt to shield their faces and traveled in closed carriages.

Young children joined their mothers in the terem but were cared for by female servants. Sons moved out of the terem when they turned four or five years old, but daughters remained. A daughter's parents arranged her marriage, which was often for political gain.

Men treated women and children according to the rigid and sometimes harsh rules in the *Domostoi*, or "house manager." This sixty-three-chapter manual, written by an adviser to Ivan the Terrible, contained guidelines on how a man should run a household and lead a good life.

Women ate their meals in the terem and talked around the samovar, or tea urn. They entertained themselves by singing and playing musical instruments.

Easter Celebration

Observation of Easter, the most important Orthodox celebration, was an important part of Moscow life. The celebration began with the Veliky Post, a seven-week-long fast, during which Orthodox believers were not allowed to eat meat, poultry, eggs, cheese, butter, milk, or sugar. People consumed dry bread, root vegetable stews, and salted fish. No weddings were performed during the Veliky Post. Ballrooms and theaters closed, and people did not entertain others in their homes. Church services were held each morning and evening.

On the eve of Easter Sunday at the stroke of midnight, families collected their Easter food and carried it to the church. After the priests blessed the food, the people carried it back home. Marking the end of Veliky Post, Easter dinner was an abundant feast. The tables in homes throughout Moscow overflowed with

After seven weeks of fasting, Easter dinner was indeed a feast.

Pashka cake

food—ham, cabbage, hard-boiled eggs, kvass, and special Easter cakes. People enjoyed *pashka*, a pyramid-shaped cake made with sweetened cottage cheese flavored with vanilla, dried fruits, and nuts. They decorated the top of the pashka with sugar and marked one side with the letters "XB," the Russian symbol for "Christ is risen." They also made *kulich*, a tall cylindrical cake with raisins, candied fruit peels, and nuts.

After the feast, the men of the family went to visit their neighbors, while the women stayed home to welcome their own visitors. The people of Moscow greeted one another by saying, "Christ is risen!" and answering, "He is risen indeed!" They then kissed each other three times and exchanged colored eggs. Street vendors did a thriving business keeping a steady supply of eggs available.

On the eve of Easter, people crowded into the church, where the priests blessed the food.

Kulich cake

Colored eggs

> *A Russian peasant is firmly persuaded that God would sooner pardon murder than a violation of Lent* [the pre-Easter season of fasting].
> —A visitor to Moscow

Wanting a gateway to Europe and a western seaport, Czar Peter the Great built a new city, Saint Petersburg, four hundred miles northwest of Moscow. He moved the capital from Moscow to Saint Petersburg in 1713. However, Moscow remained an important city and a center of industry, trade, and culture. It was often referred to as the "second capital of Russia."

Reforms of Peter the Great

After years as co-czar, Peter the Great became sole ruler of Russia in 1696. At that time, many Europeans considered Russia to be backward and barbaric. Moscow itself had changed little since the 1400s. To learn more, Peter traveled across Europe and returned ready to modernize Moscow and Russia.

Most people in Moscow were uneducated, so Peter established elementary and secondary schools in the city. He also founded a math and science school, a medical school, and an engineering school. But because these schools were mainly for the children of the upper class, the Muscovites remained largely illiterate.

Peter ended the practice of secluding women in the terem. He adopted the 12-month, 365-day Julian calendar, which the rest of Europe used. He simplified the Russian Cyrillic alphabet and had many European books translated into Russian. His work helped the first Russian newspaper begin publication. Peter funded hospitals, highways, canals, and a naval fleet. He modernized the military and made the Russian Orthodox Church a branch of the Russian government.

During his travels, Peter had noted that European men were clean-shaven, so he outlawed beards except on clergy and peasants. The Muscovites found this law so offensive that the czar eventually modified it. Peter ruled that a man could keep his beard only if he paid a "beard tax" and wore a medal with the inscription, "Beards are a ridiculous ornament."

Peter ordered men to shorten their long coats to mimic the coats of Europe. If any man refused, he was fined or forced to kneel while his coat was cut off level with the ground.

Russians resisted Peter's reforms, and the military rebelled in 1697. The next year, the czar ordered the torture and execution of one thousand members of the military. Their bodies were left swinging from the gallows in Red Square or hung on hooks from the Kremlin walls to warn others against rebellion.

Czar Peter the Great *(facing page, below)* brought European customs to Moscow. When his reforms were resisted, he had one thousand men executed *(facing page, above)*.

Winter in Moscow

The Muscovites welcomed the arrival of winter. Periods of heavy autumn rain made roads muddy and difficult to travel on. But cold winter weather froze the ground and provided a layer of snow for a smooth ride in the Russian sledges.

Several types of sledges traveled the frozen Moscow roads in winter. Wealthy boyars and nobles rode in horse-drawn sledges that looked like large wooden boxes on runners. Similar to small houses, these sledges had doors and windows and were equipped with provisions. On long trips, travelers could sleep while drivers guided the horses. Stations along the main routes allowed drivers to exchange weary horses for fresh ones.

Another type of Russian sledge was the troika. Troikas were open sleighs, made of linden bark, lined with felt, and often drawn by three horses. Travelers wrapped themselves in blankets, sheepskins, and furs to keep warm. Middle-class families hired a coachman to drive the troika. He sat on a leather stool attached to the sleigh, rested his feet upon the runners, and directed the horses with a leather whip.

The Muscovites dressed carefully for the cold weather. Their winter coats, or *shubas*, covered them to their ankles. Wealthy people owned shubas lined with sable, mink, fox fur, or bearskin. The rich wore fur caps and gloves and fur-lined boots. Poorer folks lined their shubas with sheepskin, and they wore wool hats, wool gloves, and felt boots.

Winter pastimes in Moscow included skating on frozen ponds or rivers and watching troika races. Children liked to sled down hills or ice slides—artificial hills constructed of wood and covered with ice.

In January the Muscovites gathered along the Moskva River for a special ceremony, the Blessing of the Waters. Following a procession of priests to the banks of the river, the patriarch (church bishop) and the czar mounted a platform surrounding a large hole in the ice. The priest blessed the water with prayers and incense and then sprinkled it upon the people. The Muscovites believed that the water had been made holy and would keep them safe and cure illnesses. So they filled pots with the river water and led their horses to the bank to drink. Some even dipped their children in the cold water or plunged naked into the river.

Water thrown into the air . . . freezes before it reaches the ground.
—A wintertime visitor to Moscow

Muscovites travel in troikas across a snowy landscape (*above*). Harsh winters led to deaths. Scenes of a coffin being dragged to a wintry grave (*left*) were common.

Napoleon Invades

*I*n the summer of 1812, the French leader Napoleon Bonaparte and his army of six hundred thousand men invaded Russia. Napoleon especially wanted to take over Moscow. He hoped that the rest of Russia would fall if he conquered the "second capital of Russia."

By early September, Napoleon stood on a hill overlooking Moscow, waiting for the city's leaders to surrender. While Napoleon waited, the Russian army retreated. The residents of Moscow left in carriages and on foot with cows, goats, and hen coops tied to carts. People transported works of art, icons, precious manuscripts, and jewels to the countryside for safekeeping. Of the two hundred fifty thousand residents of Moscow, only twenty thousand people remained in the city. Most were wounded soldiers, ill people, and those who could not bear to leave the city.

When Napoleon entered Moscow, he took up residence in the Kremlin and stabled his horses in the cathedrals. But one night, he and his army awoke to find that the Muscovites had set the city on fire. Strong winds fueled the flames. The French army discovered too late that the Muscovites had destroyed or removed all fire-fighting equipment. The fire raged for six days.

Napoleon, who had moved a few miles away from Moscow, wrote, "It may give you an idea of the force of the fire when I tell you that it was painful to put your palm against the walls or the windows that faced Moscow—to such an extent were they heated up. The sky and the clouds appeared to burn, it was a majestic and the most terrifying sight humanity had ever seen!"

Eventually, Napoleon and his army were forced to leave the area. The citizens of Moscow returned to find nearly seven thousand houses, one hundred twenty-two churches, and more than eight thousand businesses destroyed by the fire. The Commission for the Construction of the City of Moscow made plans to rebuild the city.

> *One saw hundreds of equipages [carriages] going through the streets, mostly full of women and children. However, the refugees occasionally included some young or old noblemen who followed the example set by the weaker sex. . . . To escape the gibes and insults of the populace, men of all ages were seen to adopt the costume of their wives and mothers, hoping by means of disguise to avoid any disagreeable comments.*
>
> —The daughter of a Moscow official, referring to the refugees who fled Moscow in Napoleon's path

Napoleon and the French army invaded Russia in 1812.

A Night at the Bolshoi

The world *bolshoi,* meaning "big" in Russian, gave the Bolshoi Ballet its name. But the famous theater had humble beginnings.

The Bolshoi troupe was founded when trustees of a Moscow orphanage started ballet classes for orphans. By the early 1800s, the company included peasant actors purchased from boyars by theater management. In 1825 the troupe moved into the huge Bolshoi Theater.

The Bolshoi staged dramas, ballets, and operas, attracting great performers from other parts of Russia and Europe. Famous artists came to design sets for the productions. The Bolshoi also developed its own unique style, which incorporated national dance and music.

Some of the most popular productions at the Bolshoi were about people and events in Russian history. Ivan the Terrible and the novel *War and Peace,*

written by Leo Tolstoy, were the subjects of many Bolshoi dramas. Guests entering the Bolshoi passed through white pillars into a grandly tiled vestibule (entryway). Marble staircases led to the main auditorium. The interior of the theater was ornately decorated with gilded carvings, and red velvet draped its six curved tiers of balconies. A special box in the center of the auditorium was reserved for the royal family.

Muscovites attending the theater dressed in fine clothing. Women wore gowns of silk, satin, or brocade and draped embroidered veils over their headdresses. Men wore black woolen dress coats, close-fitting pants, and top hats. Some dressed in their military uniforms. Coachmen drove the theatergoers to the Bolshoi in horse-drawn carts. The coachmen were not allowed inside. Instead, they passed their time gathered around fires built in small iron huts outside the theater.

Children (above) perform scenes from the ballet The Willful Wife at the Bolshoi Theater (facing page).

Struggles of the Serfs

By the 1800s, the serfs were little more than slaves to their boyar masters. No laws governed the serfs' treatment. Boyars often bought and sold their serfs like property, breaking up families in the process. Serfs could not travel or marry without their master's permission and were forbidden to own land. Boyars severely punished rebellious serfs with floggings or by deportation to Siberia. Some serfs fled to what would become modern Ukraine. Others became warriors known as Cossacks.

In the nineteenth century, serfs were forced to work in boyar-owned factories on the outskirts of Moscow. Peasants who lived on government land had to work in government-run factories. The factories required the serfs and peasants to work long hours in harsh conditions for very little pay.

Some of the czars wished to help the serfs but could not do so without angering the boyars. But after years of revolts and disorder, Czar Alexander II *(inset)* saw the need for reform. In March 1861, he abolished serfdom and freed the peasants.

Alexander II gave the peasants some personal freedoms and some land. They had to pay for the land, however, in forty-nine yearly payments—a difficult burden for most peasants. Some lost their land because they could not keep up with the payments. Many became laborers in city factories. A small number of peasants saved enough money to escape poverty. Poorer peasants resented these successful peasants, who came to be known as kulaks.

> *It is better to begin to destroy serfdom from above, than to wait until that time when it begins to destroy itself from below.*
> —Czar Alexander II

An idealistic drawing shows serfs bowing
happily to their boyar master *(above)*.

Unmarried or widowed women lived together in a barracks with their children.

The crowding and poor sanitation of factory barracks encouraged the spread of disease.

Industrialized Moscow

A majority of the industrial production in Russia during the 1800s was centered in and around Moscow. Many factories produced textiles—wool, linen, and cotton. Moscow was also an important center for transportation. By the mid-1800s, a major railroad had linked the cities of Saint Petersburg and Moscow, which had became an important distribution center for goods.

Large factories in Moscow employed up to ten thousand people. Better factories provided a church, a school, medical services, and a store for their employees. Most factories, however, had few such facilities. Workers in large factories lived in barracks—two-story wooden buildings with a yard. Unmarried men lived in one barracks, unmarried or widowed women and their children in another, and families in yet another. The barracks usually had no running water or sewage facilities. Cesspools and piles of garbage stood in the yard and streets. Workers in smaller factories had to find their own housing. Some slept on the factory floor. Diseases spread quickly in the unsanitary conditions.

Working conditions were harsh, and wages were low. A typical workday began at 6:30 A.M. and ended at 6:00 P.M. Some factories required workers to labor thirteen to seventeen hours each day. Women and children worked alongside men. The factories had little ventilation and often used strong chemicals, which caused sickness among workers.

Factory workers were unhappy with their working conditions. In 1885 a group of dissatisfied textile workers staged the first labor strike in Moscow. Although police quickly put down the strike, it laid the groundwork for future labor reform.

Coronation

In May 1896, the people of Moscow prepared for a special occasion—the coronation of Czar Nicholas II and his wife Alexandra. The ceremony lasted five hours. Nicholas took an oath to rule the country as an autocrat (supreme ruler). Bells and cannons heralded the arrival of the imperial couple at a reception.

The following day, five hundred thousand Russian people gathered to receive free food and gifts. But a rumor spread that the food and gifts would run out. The crowd panicked, and more than twelve hundred people were killed, and thousands were injured. Later that evening, Nicholas II attended a ball. Some Russians criticized him for not paying attention to their grief. The government arranged for the funerals of the dead and paid their families one thousand rubles apiece. But it was not enough to change the opinion that Nicholas was a cold-hearted ruler.

Over the next decade, different groups appealed to Nicholas II to make changes. In the countryside, the freed peasants wanted land and relief from poverty. Industrial workers wanted better working conditions. The intelligentsia, a group of artists and intellectuals, wanted a different form of government. But Nicholas II was more concerned about the health of his ill son. Influenced by his wife and a mystical healer, Rasputin, Nicholas II vowed to maintain his autocracy.

In 1905 railway workers in Moscow went on strike to protest working conditions. Workers in other industries joined them. Under pressure from the strikes, Nicholas II issued a Manifesto of Freedoms. It granted new freedoms to the population and formed a Duma, an elected legislature to approve all laws. But the Duma did little to change conditions in Russia, and the unrest continued.

Czar Nicholas II poses with his family in 1901 (*inset*). The czar (who assumed the throne in 1894) and the czarina are honored at their coronation ceremony in 1896 (*above*).

Revolution

*I*n 1914 Russia entered World War I (1914–1918). The army drafted millions of peasants and workers to fight the Central Powers (Germany and its allies). Factories that provided war materials increased production. In Moscow, residents grew suspicious of Germans living in the city's foreign quarter. They attacked German homes and businesses. Food shortages spread, and the cost of goods increased four times in three years. Bread was rationed in Moscow. Each person was allowed only one-quarter pound of bread per day. But members of the nobility went on with their lavish lives. They dined out and attended extravagant parties and balls.

In the winter of 1916, the people of Moscow demonstrated in the streets. The railway system came to a halt, and factories closed. Fuel for heating grew so scarce and expensive that only the wealthy could afford it. The police, preparing for wide-spread riots, armed themselves with machine guns.

In February 1917, telegrams brought news that a revolution was taking place in Saint Petersburg, recently renamed Petrograd. Nicholas II was forced to give up the throne, ending centuries of czarist rule. The provisional government, made up of members of the Duma, took control.

In March 1917, two soldiers travel on the footboard of a car, red flags affixed to their bayonets *(above)*. An artwork depicts Russians mourning loved ones who had been killed in the revolution *(facing page)*.

Red flags, the sign of the revolution, hung from buildings in Moscow. Workers, troops, and students marched in the streets to show their support for the new government. Revelers ripped czarist emblems from buildings and toppled statues of previous czars.

The workers of Moscow formed a *soviet*, an elected council to help keep order, ration food, and pass laws. But the provisional government did not bring peace to Russia. Different parties struggled for power. The Mensheviks, or the White Guard, wanted gradual change. The Bolsheviks, or the Red Guard, believed that the only way to bring about change was to oust the government and create a new society.

> *The Bolsheviks can and must take power into their own hands.*
> —Vladimir Lenin, Russian Communist leader

The Reds and the Whites began a struggle for power. In October 1917, fighting erupted in Moscow. Vladimir Lenin and Leon Trotsky led the Red Army through the streets and attacked the White Army. The fighting closed Moscow. People were not allowed to leave or enter the city. Shipments of food came to a standstill. The Reds eventually gained control of Moscow and seized control of Russia in 1921. Declaring Moscow to be their capital, the Reds set up headquarters in the Kremlin and changed their name to the Communist Party. In December 1922, Russia became the largest member of a new country, the Union of Soviet Socialist Republics (USSR), also known as the Soviet Union.

The Soviet symbols—the hammer and sickle and the red star—replaced the symbol of the czars, the two-headed eagle. The hammer and sickle represented the worker, and the red star stood for the Communist Party. Red stars were installed atop the Kremlin towers in 1935.

The Arrival of Communism

Vladimir Lenin and his followers believed that Communism was the answer to Russia's problems. In a Communist society, all property, goods, food, and services are owned by the government rather than by individuals or private companies. Citizens work together, and the government provides workers with a job, an income, shelter, education, and health care.

Lenin abolished class distinctions by removing titles from the nobility and army officials. The government took control of all land, livestock, industry, homes, and stores. In the countryside, government officials assigned peasants to large farms. The practice of religion was forbidden. To maintain order and to destroy his enemies, Lenin set up the Checka, a secret police force that was ordered to find, arrest, and shoot counterrevolutionary troublemakers.

Although many Russians believed in Lenin's ideals, hardships continued after the revolution. The bread ration in Moscow fell to a meager one-eighth pound per day for each person. Crime, starvation, and deadly diseases spread throughout the city. People begged and bartered on the streets to try to get the

Vladimir Lenin addresses a crowd in 1918 *(above)*. A 1920 Russian poster depicts the hard work done by the Russian people *(facing page)*.

necessities of life. To ease the situation, Lenin allowed *nepmen*, small business owners, to run private shops and services.

Lenin died in 1924, and despite freezing temperatures, thousands of Muscovites lined up to view Lenin's body. Millions of Russians crowded the streets to pay their respects as his casket was escorted through the city by other Communist leaders. Lenin's successors ordered his body preserved and displayed inside a tomb built in Red Square. The government renamed the city of Petrograd Leningrad in Lenin's honor.

Apartment Living

The population of Moscow exploded in the first half of the twentieth century. A severe housing shortage led Soviet leaders to build more apartments. The typical apartment block design consisted of four steel-and-concrete buildings, six to eight stories tall. The buildings stood around a central courtyard or playground. Individual apartments had four to five rooms.

New construction didn't end the housing problems. People were forced to share living quarters. Apartments originally intended to house single families became home to many families. Each family, no matter its size, was confined to one room. The hallway, kitchen, and bathroom were shared by all. By 1925 eighty-five thousand Muscovites were living in a space with more than eight persons per room. Communal apartments were cramped, and family relationships were strained.

To buy food, clothing, or other items, Muscovites had to stand in long lines nearly every day. Because both fathers and mothers worked outside the home, babushkas (grandmothers) usually took over the family shopping, cleaning, cooking, and child care.

To get away from the crowded conditions and stress of life in Moscow, many families escaped to dachas, or country cottages. The Soviet government ordered citizens to use their dachas to grow much of the food themselves to ease the government's burden of providing for them. Some wealthy Muscovites had lavish dachas along the Black Sea. But the average dacha was in a village ten miles outside of Moscow. Nearby woods provided wild berries and mushrooms. Although most dachas had no electricity, hot water, or toilets, Muscovites spent as much time there as they could.

Grandmothers waited in long lines to buy food.

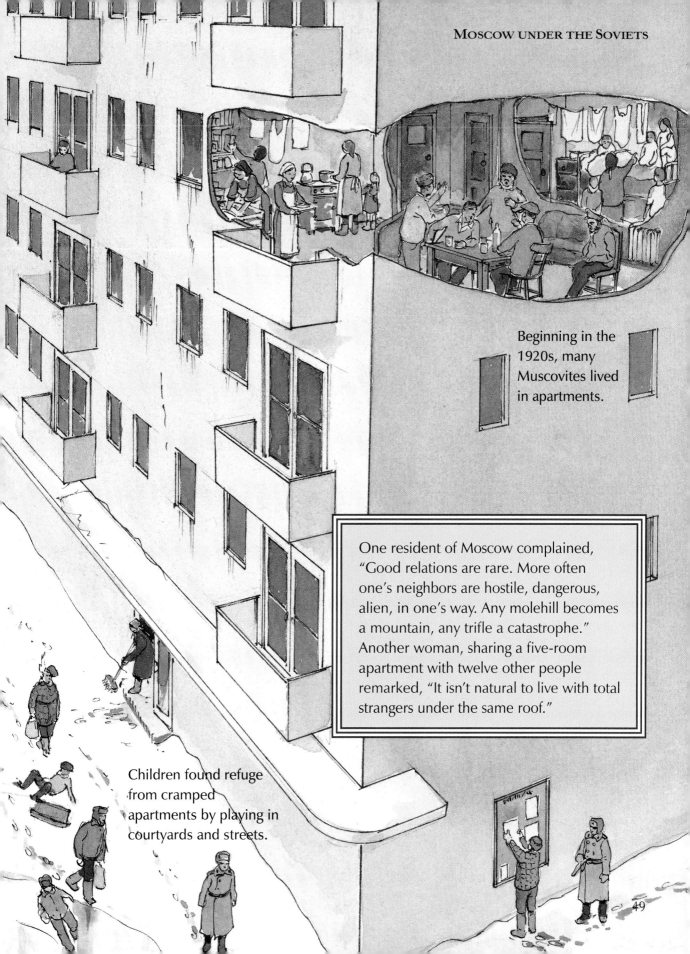

Beginning in the 1920s, many Muscovites lived in apartments.

One resident of Moscow complained, "Good relations are rare. More often one's neighbors are hostile, dangerous, alien, in one's way. Any molehill becomes a mountain, any trifle a catastrophe." Another woman, sharing a five-room apartment with twelve other people remarked, "It isn't natural to live with total strangers under the same roof."

Children found refuge from cramped apartments by playing in courtyards and streets.

The Terror of Stalin

Joseph Stalin became the leader of the Soviet Union after Lenin's death. Stalin had a vision for the social and economic transformation of Russia. He hoped to increase farm production, expand industry, modernize cities, and bolster the military. But his plan involved seizing all food produced on farms. In protest, farmers destroyed about half of the Soviet Union's livestock and produce. Millions of peasants starved to death or fled to the city to seek jobs in factories. Forced to meet government quotas (production goals), workers became little more than slave laborers. Large construction projects, including the Moscow subway system, modernized the capital. But many of the laborers who built the system died in accidents caused by poor working conditions.

The character of Moscow changed. Stalin ordered churches demolished or transformed into warehouses, stores, and public bathrooms. Restaurants in Moscow became communal dining rooms.

Stalin grew suspicious of people disloyal to the government. He ordered the Checka to arrest anyone suspected of being anti-Soviet.

In Moscow the Checka searched homes and arrested thousands of citizens.

During the late 1930s, one million people were executed under Stalin's orders. Another fifteen million were arrested and sent to forced labor camps in Siberia. Lubyanka, the Checka headquarters, became the most well-known prison in Moscow. Many times an arrest had no real cause. A person could be charged with being a member of a traitor's family or a friend of a traitor. A survivor of Stalin's terror says, "There was a joke in those years. A new man arrives in the cell. 'How long did you get?' everyone asks. 'Fifteen years,' he says. 'For what?' 'For nothing.' 'Couldn't be. For nothing they give ten.'"

Shoppers bargain at a meat stall in 1932 *(facing page)*. People line up to exchange ration cards for bread *(right)*. The Moscow Sukharvsky market bustles with activity *(below)*.

Young Pioneers

Soviet leaders wanted Russian children to grow up to become productive members of the Communist Party. So the government formed Communist youth groups. Training in the ways of Communism started at age eight, when a child could become a Young Octobrist. Young Octobrists wore star-shaped pins with a picture of Lenin as a child. They learned how to be good Soviet citizens. They were taught that loyalty to the Communist Party was more important than anything, even family. Some children betrayed their parents to the authorities.

After their tenth birthday, children could join the Young Pioneers. Prospective members formed a horseshoe and recited the promise of the Young Pioneers—to be good friends and good citizens. They stated the Young Pioneer motto, "Always ready!" Stepping forward one at a time, each child received a red scarf and a pin with a picture of Lenin as a young man.

Members of the Young Pioneers participated in after-school activities at the Young Pioneers Palace in Moscow. In the summer, they went to government-run camps to swim, boat, and hike.

In the spring, Young Pioneers marched in the annual May Day Parade. May Day (May 1) celebrated the military, laborers, and students. The entire city prepared for the celebration, decorating buildings with balloons, red streamers, and Soviet flags. GUM, a large shopping center across from Red Square, and other buildings were draped with banners of political leaders. Vendors sold food and souvenirs from kiosks, or booths.

On the morning of May 1, marchers assembled along the side of the Moskva River to await the start of the parade. The highest-ranking officials of the Communist Party watched the parade from atop Lenin's tomb in Red Square.

Tanks, missiles, and soldiers proceeded through Red Square. The civilian parade followed, with factory workers and members of sports clubs. Then came hundreds of Young Pioneers dressed in matching blue pants or skirts, white shirts, and red scarves. Planes flew overhead, dipping their wings in salute to the Communist officials. At the end of the busy day, people gathered to watch a spectacular fireworks display.

In 1919 Moscow's young people assemble to celebrate the anniversary of the revolution *(facing page)*. Russian children *(below)* wave flags during a 1924 May Day celebration in Red Square.

Moscow's air-raid shelters were in the city's subway stations. The stations, decorated with mosaics of Soviet life, had adequate bathrooms. Women and children huddled on the platforms of the stations, while men gathered in the tunnels where trains normally ran. Muscovites spent many nights in shelters. They hurried to them at nightfall when the air-raid alarms sounded. People went home at the "all clear" signal in the early morning.

Muscovites dug antitank ditches in 1941 (*above*). City residents took shelter in the Moscow subway (*left*) during Nazi air raids.

World War II

During World War II (1939–1945), German leader Adolf Hitler led the Nazi army in a three-pronged attack against the cities of Leningrad, Kiev, and Moscow. Moscow was a major industrial source of weapons and ammunition and a key to railway communications.

On July 15, 1941, Nazi bombs began falling on Moscow, leaving craters in Red Square. People fled to underground air-raid shelters built into subways. The Nazis dropped bombs designed to spread fire. Some Muscovites volunteered to stand on rooftops to watch for fires during the bombings. At the first sign of fire, the fire department rushed to put out the blaze. In addition, officials ordered blackouts, which meant all lights had to be turned off at night. False rooftops were painted on the ground around the Kremlin to trick the Nazi bombers. Women helped dig trenches to the west of Moscow to hamper the advance of the Nazi forces.

The government strictly rationed supplies. Food shortages increased. Factories produced goods for the military instead of for consumers, so there was little to buy. It was illegal to use electricity for cooking. The city's heating system did not work due to a lack of fuel. Many people built temporary wood-burning stoves called *vremyankas*.

Late in July 1941, the government authorized the evacuation of Moscow. Many families moved east. Factory machines were taken apart and loaded onto railcars and then shipped eastward to the Ural Mountains, where they were reassembled. The government relocated offices outside of Moscow, but Stalin remained in the Kremlin. On October 16, 1941, a rumor spread that the Nazis had broken through Russian defenses north of Moscow, and more people fled. Of Moscow's 4.5 million residents, only 2.5 million stayed in the city.

Weather came to the city's aid. October brought thick mud, known as the *rasputitza*. The knee-deep mud bogged down German military equipment and slowed the advance of Hitler's army. When the temperature plunged to −30°F, armor and weapons froze into the ground. The Nazis were not prepared for winter. They had no winter clothing and no antifreeze or winter oil for their equipment. Even so, Hitler's troops came within sight of the Kremlin before the Russian army stopped their advance. By early 1942, the Germans had began to retreat.

Another Revolution

The 1950s and the 1960s in the Soviet Union were times of relative peace. The Soviet premier (leader) Nikita Khrushchev introduced more freedoms and worked to raise the country's standard of living. But after he was overthrown in 1964, the nation experienced food shortages, corruption, and oppression under the rule of Krushchev's successors.

When Mikhail Gorbachev became Soviet premier in 1985, he attempted to reform the economy through a policy called *perestroika.* Gorbachev welcomed *glasnost,* or freedom and openness of expression. He encouraged people to own land and businesses.

Despite Gorbachev's efforts, the economy declined. Inflation (a continuing rise in prices) increased, and the Soviet people grew more and more disillusioned.

On August 19, 1991, a coup (overthrow of the government) was staged. Tanks rolled into Moscow. The morning news declared, "Vice President Gennady Yanayev has taken over the duties of president of the USSR . . . due to Mikhail Gorbachev's inablity to perform his duties."

Eight opponents of Gorbachev had taken over the Kremlin and had formed an emergency committee. Outside the Russian Parliament, Boris Yeltsin, the president of Russia (the largest Soviet republic), denounced the coup. Protesters built barricades around the building, using vehicles, fences, tree trunks, bathtubs, wooden desks, and mattresses.

The demonstrators linked arms to form a human chain to keep troops away. Yeltsin mounted a tank and addressed the one hundred fifty thousand citizens, calling for defiance of the Emergency Committee.

On the night of August 20, 1991, three demonstrators were killed. Nervously, the crowd held its position. By the next day, the Emergency Committee realized the coup had failed. Tanks and the troops pulled out of Moscow, and the leaders of the coup were arrested.

By November 1991, most Soviet republics had declared independence. In early December, Yeltsin and other leaders announced the formation of the Commonwealth of Independent States (a loose association of some of the former Soviet republics). Gorbachev resigned as Soviet premier in late December, and the Soviet Union was officially dissolved.

Premier Nikita Khrushchev in 1959 (*left, above*). More than thirty years later, crowds applaud the toppling of the statue of Lenin (*right, above*). Soviet tanks assume position during the 1991 coup (*below*). President Boris Yeltsin addresses a crowd (*left*).

Modern-Day Moscow

In 1992 Boris Yeltsin announced his plan to transform Russia's economic system into a capitalist system (in which individuals own goods and land). Most businesses would be owned by private citizens who were free to make a profit from their work. The needs of the market, not the government, would determine production levels.

Capitalism was slow to come to some parts of Russia, but it came about quickly in Moscow. By the mid-1990s, shopping malls and international restaurant chains appeared. Neon signs and billboards advertised foreign brands and American movies. People sold imported electronics and sportswear in open-air markets. New fashion styles appeared in store windows. The number of cars in the city doubled. Businesspeople grew prosperous in the new economy. Many newly rich citizens drove luxury cars.

Other changes marked the revolution. Streets that had been renamed after the 1917 takeover were renamed yet again. Many buildings were restored to their previous glory. Churches were rebuilt, and Muscovites were welcome to worship again.

The majority of Muscovites, however,

(*From left*) Moscow's GUM department store attracts visitors from far and wide; a babushka sells flowers outside a fifteen-story apartment building; young people hang out in Red Square.

grew poorer and more desperate. Artists, composers, and writers could no longer count on government support to help them live. Thousands of people had to work second and third jobs to make ends meet. Crime increased as law enforcement weakened.

In August 1998, Russia suffered a severe economic setback. A falling income hampered Russia's ability to pay its large foreign debt. Wages went unpaid, banks failed, and people's savings evaporated. Goods disappeared from store shelves. The continuing financial crisis threatened political stability as Yeltsin lost public support. He resigned on December 31, 1999.

Yeltsin named Vladimir Putin, the former head of Russia's Federal Security Service, as his successor. The people of Russia elected him president in March 2000.

Moscow continues to play an important role as the economic, cultural, and religious center of the Russian Federation (Russia). The famous nineteenth-century Russian poet Aleksandr Pushkin summed up the feelings of the people when he wrote, "Moscow—to Russian hearts how much it means! How many memories [it] redeems!"

Moscow Timeline

	First Millennium B.C.	First and Second Millennium A.D.
3000 B.C.–A.D. 988 **Early History**	**3000 B.C.** **C. 1000 B.C.**	Neolithic (polished stone tool culture) settlements appear in parts of Russia Finns settle in northern Russia
		A.D. 400–500 Slavs expand into northern Russia and intermingle with Finns **A.D. 862** Russian territories unite under Rurik **A.D. 988** Prince Vladimir of Kiev introduces Christianity to Russia
A.D. 1100–1302 **Early Moscow**		**C. A.D. 1100** Village of Kuchkovo built on the Moskva River **A.D. 1147** First mention of Moscow in the *Ipatievskaya* **A.D. 1156** First kremlin built **A.D. 1237** Mongol invasion; Moscow destroyed; beginning of Mongol Yoke
A.D. 1302–1462 **The Growth of Moscow**		**A.D. 1327** Head of the Russian Orthodox Church moves to Moscow **A.D. 1453** Fall of Constantinople; Moscow becomes the "Third Rome"
A.D. 1462–1682 **Moscow under the Czars**		**A.D. 1462** Ivan the Great comes to power **A.D. 1547** Ivan the Terrible crowned as czar **A.D. 1598–1613** The Time of Troubles **A.D. 1601–1603** Severe famines in Moscow **A.D. 1610–1612** Poles occupy Moscow **A.D. 1613** Foreign Quarter moved outside city limits; Mikhail Romanov elected czar, founds dynasty **A.D. 1649** Laws bind peasants to land as serfs

Second Millennium A.D.

A.D. 1682–1861 **Modernizing Moscow**	**A.D. 1687–1701**	Institutions of higher education established in Moscow
	A.D. 1696	Peter the Great becomes sole czar
	1700s A.D.	First industries set up in Moscow
	A.D. 1703	First Russian newspaper published in Moscow
	A.D. 1713	The capital is transferred from Moscow to Saint Petersburg
	A.D. 1773	Founding of Bolshoi Ballet
	A.D. 1812	Napoleon invades Moscow; most of city destroyed by fire
	A.D. 1851	First major railroad in Russia links Moscow to Saint Petersburg
A.D. 1861–1917 **Rumblings of** **Revolution**	**A.D. 1861**	Alexander II frees the serfs
	A.D. 1861–1891	Cotton industry quadruples in Moscow
	A.D. 1896	Coronation of Nicholas II
	A.D. 1897–1915	Population of Moscow doubles to two million
	A.D. 1905	Labor strikes; Nicholas II issues Manifesto of Freedoms; formation of Duma
	A.D. 1914	Russia enters World War I
	A.D. 1916	Widespread demonstrations call for "land, peace, bread"
	A.D. 1917	The February Revolution—Nicholas II abdicates The October Revolution—Bolsheviks, under Lenin, seize control of Moscow
A.D. 1917–1985 **Moscow under** **the Soviets**	**A.D. 1917–1921**	Civil war between the Bolsheviks and Mensheviks
	A.D. 1918	Lenin returns the capital to Moscow
	A.D. 1924	Lenin dies; Stalin comes to power
	A.D. 1926–1939	Population of Moscow grows to four million
	A.D. 1935–1941	Stalin executes or exiles millions
	A.D. 1939	World War II begins
	A.D. 1941	Nazi forces attack Moscow
	A.D. 1953	Stalin dies
A.D. 1985– **The Fall of** **Communism**	**A.D. 1985**	Mikhail Gorbachev appointed head of Communist Party
	A.D. 1986	Gorbachev's reforms of *perestroika* and *glasnost*
	A.D. 1991	Attempted coup fails; Boris Yeltsin comes to power; end of Communist rule; Soviet Union dissolved
	A.D. 1998	Economic crisis in Russia
	A.D. 1999	Yeltsin resigns and names Vladimir Putin as his successor
	A.D. 2000	Putin officially elected as Russia's president

Books about Russia and Moscow

Brewster, Hugh. *Anastasia's Album.* New York: Hyperion Books for Children, 1996.

Buettner, Dan. *Sovietrek: A Journey by Bicycle across Russia.* Minneapolis: Lerner Publications Company, 1994.

Gray, Bettyanne. *Manya's Story: Faith and Survival in Revolutionary Russia.* Minneapolis: Runestone Press, 1995.

Haskins, Jim. *Count Your Way through Russia.* Minneapolis: Carolrhoda Books, Inc., 1987.

Haviland, Virginia. *Favorite Fairy Tales Told in Russia.* New York: Beech Tree Books, 1995.

Holmes, Burton. *Moscow.* Philadelphia: Chelsea House, 1998.

Kossman, Nina. *Behind the Border.* New York: Lothrop, Lee and Shepard Books, 1994.

Leder, Jane Mersky. *A Russian Jewish Family.* Minneapolis: Lerner Publications Company, 1996.

Murrell, Kathleen Berton. *Russia.* London: Dorling Kindersley Ltd., 1998.

Nadel, Laurie. *The Kremlin Coup.* Brookfield, CT: The Millbrook Press, 1992.

Russia (Then and Now). Minneapolis: Lerner Publications Company, 1986.

Sherrow, Victoria. *Life during the Russian Revolution.* San Diego: Lucent Books, 1998.

Streissguth, Tom. *Russia (Globe-trotters Club).* Minneapolis: Carolrhoda Books, Inc., 1997.

Index

About the Author and Illustrator

Patricia Toht has been writing for children for more than a decade and owned a children's bookstore for seven years. She is an avid collector of children's literature and likes to travel. She lives in Wheaton, Illinois, with her husband, Don, and four children.

Bob Moulder of Derby, England, studied art in Belfast, Northern Ireland. He is a specialist in historical artwork and comic strips. He currently works with the Oxford Illustrators and Designers group.

Acknowledgments

For quoted material: p. 26, Nicholas V. Riasanovsky. *A History of Russia.* (New York: Oxford University Press, 1993); p. 29, Eugene Anschel. *The American Image of Russia, 1775–1825.* (New York: Frederick Ungar Publishing Co., 1974); p. 33, Anthony Cross. *Russia Under Western Eyes, 1517–1825.* (New York: St. Martin's Press, 1971); p. 34, William Klein, et. al. *Moscow.* (Boston: Houghton Mifflin, 1997); p. 35, Antony Brett-James. *1812.* (New York: St. Martin's Press, 1966); p. 38, Jerome Blum. *Lord and Peasant in Russia.* (Princeton, NJ: Princeton University Press, 1961); p. 45, Michael Gibson. *The Russian Revolution.* (East Sussex, England: Wyland Publishers Ltd., 1986); p. 49, quote #1, Andrei Sinyavsky. *Soviet Civilization, A Cultural History.* (New York: Arcade Publishing, 1988); p. 49, quote #2, Richard Lourie. *Russia Speaks.* (New York: HarperCollins, 1991); p. 50, Richard Lourie. *Russia Speaks.* New York: HarperCollins, 1991, p. 173–74; p. 58, David Remnick. "Moscow: The New Revolution." (*National Geographic,* vol. 191, no. 4, April 1997).

For photographs/and fine art reproductions: © Barry Lewis/Stone, p. 5 (top); © Glen Allison/Stone, p. 5 (bottom); *The Life of St. Sergius of Radonezh,* (15th century), Private Collection/Index/Bridgeman Art Library, p. 14; The Granger Collection, pp. 15, 17 (top); Stock Montage, Inc., p. 17 (bottom); Russian State Museum, St. Petersburg, Russia (Gosudarstvenni Russky Musei)/Leonid Bogdanov/SuperStock, p. 18; *Tsar Ivan IV Vasilyevich 'the Terrible,' (1530–84),* 1897 Victor Mikhailovich Vasnetsov (1848–1926), Tretyakov Gallery, Moscow, Russia/Bridgeman Art Library, p. 25 (top); North Wind Picture Archives, pp. 25 (bottom), 38, 39; *The Morning of the Execution of the Streltsy in 1698,* 1881 by Vasili Ivanovich Surikov/Tretyakov Gallery, Moscow, Russia/Bridgeman Art Library, p. 30 (top); Historical Museum, Moscow, Russia/ET Archive, London/SuperStock, p. 30 (bottom); Russian State Museum, St. Petersburg, Russia/SuperStock, p. 33 (top); *Seeing off the Dead,* 1865 by Vasili Grigorevich Perov, Tretyakov Gallery, Moscow, Russia/Bridgeman Art Library, p. 33 (bottom); *Battle of Moscow, 7 September 1812, 1822* (oil on canvas) by Louis Lejeune (1775–1848), Chateau de Versailles, France/Reunion des Musees Nationaux/Bridgeman Art Library, p. 35; SOVFOTO, p. 36; SOVFOTO/EASTFOTO, pp. 37, 46; Stock Montage/Superstock, p. 42; Giraudon/Art Resource, NY, p. 43; Archive Photos, p. 44; *Death in Snow,* 1905 by Vladimir Egorovich Makovsky, Central Museum of the Revolution, Moscow, Russia/Novosti/Bridgeman Art Library, p. 45; Archive Photos, p. 47; ITAR-TASS/SOVFOTO, pp. 50, 51 (top), 51 (bottom); Corbis/Bettmann-UPI, p. 52; © Liaison, p. 53; SOVFOTO, p. 54 (top), 54 (bottom); Archive Photos, p. 57 (top left); Reuters/Corbis, p. 57 (top right), 57 (center), 57 (bottom); © David Sutherland/Stone, p. 58; © Buck Kelly/Liaison Agency, p. 59 (left); © Alain Le Garsmeur/Stone, p. 59 (right). Cover: © Glen Allison/Stone.